You...

I wanted to show my appreciation that you support my work so I've put together a free gift for you.

OUTDOOR COOKING ESSENTIALS
Top 25 Camping Food & BBQ Recipes

http://thezenfactory.com/california_texas_free_book/

Just visit the link above to download it now.

I know you will love this gift.

California Smoker Recipes:

Essential TOP 25 Meat Recipes

by Daniel Hinkle, Marvin Delgado, Ralph Replogle

California Smoker Recipes: 2
Introduction 6
Barbecue California Style 8
Direct Vs. Indirect Grilling 9
- Direct Grilling or Barbecuing 9
- Indirect Grilling or Barbecuing 9
- Combination Grilling or Barbecuing 10

Bacon 11
- Ingredients: 11
- Directions: 11

Smoked Standing Rib Roast 13
- Ingredients: 13
- Directions: 13

Smoked Steelhead Trout Salmon 15
- Ingredients: 15
- Directions: 15

Smoked Pork Butt 17
- Ingredients: 17
- Directions: 17

Honey Smoked Turkey 19
- Ingredients: 19
- Directions: 20

Alder Pan Smoked Salmon 21
- Ingredients: 21
- Directions: 21

Mouth Watering Beef Jerky 23
- Ingredients: 23

Directions:	24
Crispy Grilled Pizza Margherita	25
Ingredients:	25
Directions:	25
Grilled Zucchini	27
Ingredients:	27
Directions:	27
Smoked Asparagus	29
Ingredients:	29
Directions:	30
Smoked Herb Chicken	31
Ingredients:	31
Directions:	32
Bodacious Barbecue Ribs	33
Ingredients:	33
Directions:	34
Northern California Smoked Brisket	35
Ingredients:	35
Directions:	36
Hot Smoked California Yellowtail	37
Ingredients:	37
Directions:	37
California Avocado-Smoked Corn & Crab Bisque with Avocado-Chive Oil	39
Ingredients:	39
Directions:	40
California Smoked Salmons Sushi Roll	42

Ingredients:	42
Directions:	43
California BBQ Chicken Pizza	44
Ingredients:	44
Directions:	45
Smoked California Avocado Butter Trout Toast	46
Ingredients:	46
Directions:	47
Smoked Tri Tip	48
Ingredients:	48
Directions:	48
	50
California Avocado, Egg and Smoked Salmon Blini	50
Ingredients:	50
Directions:	51
California Club Smoked Turkey Quesadilla	53
Ingredients:	53
Directions:	53
Soupe a l'oignongratinee	55
Ingredients:	55
Directions:	56
Turkey Smoker	57
Ingredients:	57
Directions:	58
Grilled Lamb Sausage with Cheese, Tomatoes, and Herbs	59
Ingredients:	59
Directions:	60

California Honey BBQ Sauce 61
    Ingredients: 61
    Directions: 62
Southern California Barbecue sauce 63
    Ingredients: 63
    Directions: 64
Conclusion 65

Introduction

California is a place where you can easily get lost in the waves and sunshine. Many people think about visiting California for the seafood, but they rarely contemplate visiting for the seafood or the smoked barbecue. However, California is well known for their smoked seafood and for their delicious barbecued chunks of meat and vegetables.

Because there are a large number of people from California who have joined the vegetarian way of life, we have included plenty of vegetarian based recipes that are sure to tickle your taste buds just as much as the traditional smoked meat recipes.

We guarantee that you will love the meat and vegetable based recipes equally. Thought you didn't like your vegetables? We bet you change your mind when you taste our delicious grilled and smoked morsels.

Barbecue California Style

California barbecue focuses on locally grown fruits, vegetables and meats. Many of the recipes are centered on locally harvested fish and seafood and there is a large focus on including meats and vegetables in their recipes and not just focusing on a single product.

California barbecue also has a strong focus on the use of beer as a moisturizing agent in the recipes, as it gives great flavor and ensures that the meat stays deliciously moist and scrumptious.

We hope you enjoy the amazing recipes that we have included in this book. We have packed 25 delicious California barbeque, grill and smoked recipes into this book that - while we love our readers – we didn't want to share with anyone else. However, we could not keep the delicious flavors all to ourselves any longer.

Direct Vs. Indirect Grilling

There is more to barbecuing and grilling than simply selecting the best ingredients. You must also make yourself familiar with the three main variations of grilling – direct, indirect, and combination.

The direct cooking method cooks food with direct influence from the heat or flame.

The indirect method cooks by using reflected heat. The food is placed in a box with heat, but it never has direct contact with the flame source.

Combination Cooking is just as it sounds, a combination of the two main cooking methods.

Direct Grilling or Barbecuing

The direct method of grilling and barbecuing is used for searing foods and cooking foods that take less than 20 minutes to finish cooking. In this category would be shrimp, burgers, pork chops, lamb chops and steaks.

This method can be completed on almost any grill or barbecue. It is most effective if the lid of the grill is closed as this creates a convection type cooking atmosphere.

Indirect Grilling or Barbecuing

This method of grilling, barbecuing or smoking is typically reserved for large cuts of meat. These meats require being cooked at a lower temperature for a longer duration of time. The food does not come into contact with direct heat or flame. Instead, a reflective type cooking is used. In order to accomplish this, the lid of the grill MUST be closed at all times.

Using the indirect grilling or barbecuing method requires you to have proper knowledge of adding soaked smoking woods or briquettes to the grill every hour to keep a low, smoldering fire going at a constant temperature.

Combination Grilling or Barbecuing

This method of grilling is literally a combination of the previous mentioned methods. Typically the food is seared over a direct flame and then the food is transferred to a cooler portion of the grill to cook the remaining duration. This method is perfect for any meat that you wish to obtain a caramelized exterior, with a tender, juicy interior.

Bacon

(ready in about 6 days | Servings 4 pounds bacon)

Ingredients:

- 4 pounds raw pork belly
- ½ cup brown sugar, packed
- ¼ cup sugar-based curing mixture
- 1 gallon cold water
- 1 (10 pound) bag charcoal
- Hickory or apple wood chips

Directions:

1. Using a 2 gallon container, combine the brown sugar, water and curing mixture. Submerge pork belly in mixture. Weigh down any meat that rises using a dinner plate/ Refrigerate covered for six days.

2. Light the charcoal using an outdoor smoker. Soak the wood chips in a large bowl of water. Once temperature of smoker reaches 140-150 degrees F, the coals are then ready. Smoke the pork belly meat for approx. 6 hours, replenish the wood chips every hour during the process. Chill in refrigerator. Slice and serve fried.

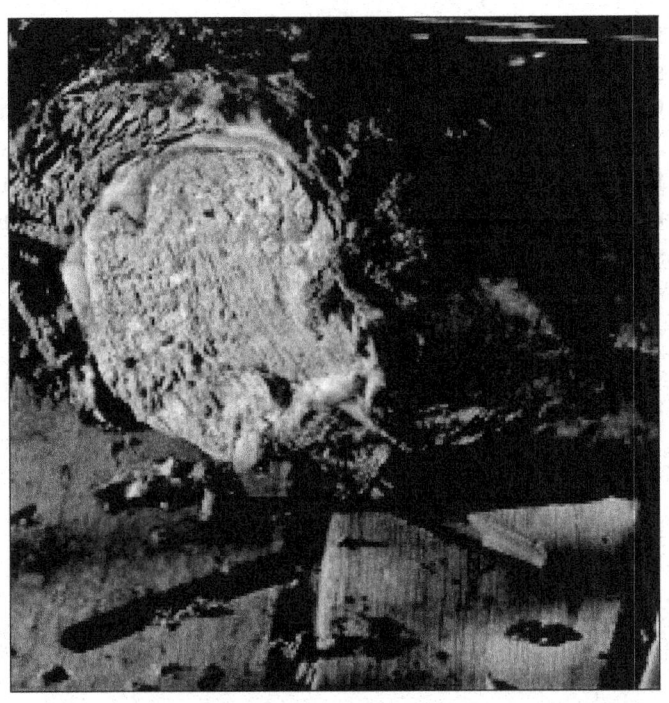

Smoked Standing Rib Roast
(ready in about 10hours | Serving 6)

Ingredients:
- 15 pounds charcoal briquettes
- 2 pounds hickory wood chips
- 1 cup bourbon whiskey
- 1 (4 pound) rib roast, bone intact
- ½ cup steak seasoning

Directions:
1. Start 10 pounds of charcoal, torpedo style smoker. Start a hot fire, fill secondary pan with cold water and allow coals to

turn white. Soak hickory chips in bourbon. Rub roast with the steak seasoning, ensuring that all surfaces are coated.
2. Once the coals are ready, place the roast on the top grate. Throw numerous handfuls of soaked hickorychips into the fire, close the lid. Check fire regularly every 45 minutes, add more charcoal to keep flame alive. Cook for 8-10 hours, meat should be 145 degrees F in the center once finished.

Smoked Steelhead Trout Salmon
(ready in about 13 hours | Servings 6)

Ingredients:

- 2 pounds steelhead trout fillets
- 2 tbsp. olive oil
- 4 chopped garlic cloves
- 1 ½ tbsp. dried rosemary, crushed
- 1 cup sugar-based curing mixture
- 1 quarter of water
- Ground black pepper
- 1 pound alder wood chips, soaked in wine or water

Directions:
1. Rinse fish fillets and place in shallow (preferably glass) baking dish. Drizzle oil over the fish and season with

rosemary and garlic. Rub seasonings well into the fish. Cover and chill overnight
2. Dissolve curing salt in water and pour into shallow dish, fish intact. Allow to marinate for 15 minutes.
3. Prepare the smoker to operate for 4 hours on slow burn, use charcoal. Temperature should be at 150 degrees F prior to cooking.
4. Transfer fish from brine and cover each piece with aluminum foil, season with pepper for tasting. Place each piece onto rack and sprinkle soaked wood chips over the coal. Cover and smoke for 2 hours, replenish if required.
5. Increase temperature to 200 degrees F and continue to smoke until internal temperature of fish reaches 165 degrees F. Remove from smoker, rest for 20 minutes and serve.

Smoked Pork Butt
(ready in about 1 day 12 hours 20 mins | Servings 16)

Ingredients:

- 7 pounds of fresh pork butt roast
- 2 tbsp. ground New Mexico chile powder
- 4 tbsp. brown sugar, packed

Directions:

1. Soak pork butt in brine solution for 4 hours (or overnight), covered in the refrigerator
2. Preheat outdoor smoker to 200-225 degrees F
3. Use a small bowl to combine brown sugar, chili powder and additional seasoning, if desired. Apply to the meat and season well, rubbing in with your fingers. Allocate roasting rack above a drip pan and transfer meat to the rack
4. Smoke at 200-225 degrees F for 6-18 hours, depending on preference. Internal heat of pork should reach 145 degrees F prior to completion

Honey Smoked Turkey

(ready in about 3 hours 45 minutes | Servings 1 (12pound) turkey)

Ingredients:

- 1 whole turkey
- 2 tbsp. fresh sage, chopped
- 2tbsp. ground black pepper
- 2 tbsp. celery salt
- 2 tbsp. fresh basil, chopped
- 2 tbsp. vegetable oil

- 1 (12 ounce) jar of honey
- ½ pound of mesquite wood chips

Directions:

1. Preheat grill to high heat. If using charcoal grill, use twice the regular amount. Soak wood chips in water and place next to grill
2. Remove giblets and neck from turkey. Rinse well and pat dry. Transfer to a large roasting pan.
3. Mix together black pepper, sage, basil, celery salt and vegetable oil in a medium bowl. Pour mixture over turkey evenly. Place the turkey breast side down into the pan, tent and cover with aluminum foil.
4. Move roasting pan into the preheated grill. Throw handfuls of wood chips into the coals. Cover and cook for 1 hour.
5. Throw 2 more handfuls of wood chips into the fire. Drizzle honey over the turkey and replace the foil. Cover grill and cook for further 1 ½-2 hours. Internal temperature should reach 180 degrees F.
6. Remove foil from turkey and turn breast side up in roasting pan. Baste with any leftover honey and allow to cook, uncovered, for 15 minutes. Serve once honey is very dark.

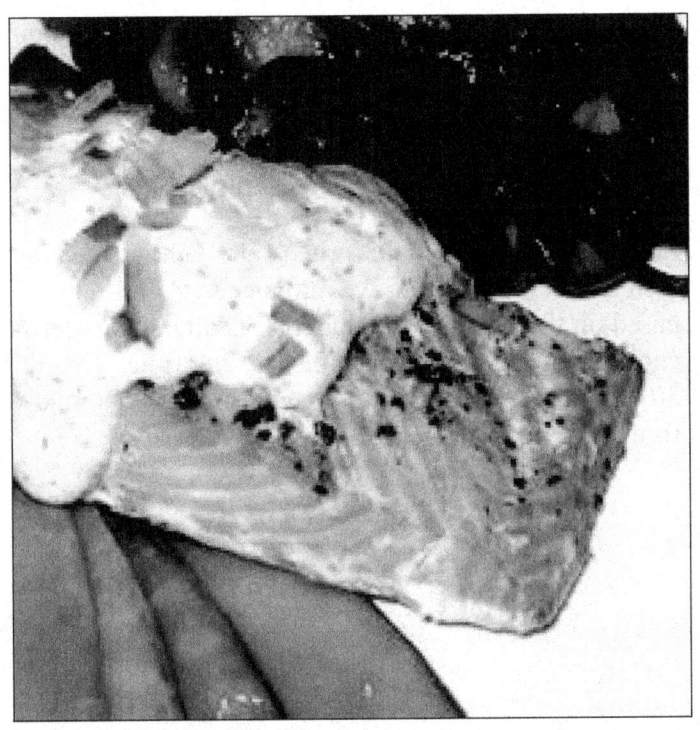

Alder Pan Smoked Salmon
(ready in about 10 hours | Serving 10)

Ingredients:

- 1 (3 pound) salmon fillet
- Fresh ground black pepper
- 1/8 cup brown sugar, packed
- ½ tsp. salt
- 1 tbsp. water

Directions:

1. Soak salmon fillet in premade brine solution for 4 hours, or overnight. Submerge alder wood plank in water.
2. Preheat outdoor smoker to 160-180 degrees F.
3. Transfer salmon from brine to cold running water, rinse well. Pat dry and remove wood plank from water, lay fish onto the plank. Season with black pepper.
4. Smoke salmon for 2 hours, check at 1 ½ hours just in case. Fish should be able to flake into pieces. Adjust cooking time based on the amount of reduction of salt content during cooking, as salt content diminishes over time.
5. 30 minutes before fish is done, mix brown sugar and water to form paste. Brush over the salmon and serve.

Mouth Watering Beef Jerky
(ready in about 18 hours | Serving 12)

Ingredients:

- 5 pounds boneless beef sirloin
- 2 cups soy sauce
- 1 cup water
- 3 dashes Worcestershire sauce
- 3 tbsp. white sugar (optional)
- 3 tbsp. salt
- ½ tsp. onion powder
- ¼ tsp. garlic powder
- 2 tsp. liquid smoke flavoring

- Mesquite or hickory wood chips

Directions:
1. Cut beef into ¼ inch thick slices. In a small bowl combine water, soy sauce, Worcestershire sauce, salt, sugar, garlic powder, onion powder and liquid smoke. Pour mixture into heavy duty re-sealable bag. Add beef and combine well; seal and chill for 12 hours
2. Remove beef from bag and pat dry, allow to sit for 30 minutes. Discard marinade and soak wood chips in preparation for cooking
3. Preheat smoker prior to cooking
4. Arrange beef into drying racks. Smoke for 5-7 hours, replenish wood chips when required.

Crispy Grilled Pizza Margherita

(ready in about 1 hour 35 minutes | Serving 6)

Ingredients:

- 1 (16 ounce) pizza dough package, room temperature
- ¼ cup olive oil
- 4ounces shredded Asiago cheese
- 3 thinly sliced large tomatoes
- 1 cup whole basil leaves, packed
- 8 ounces fresh mozzarella cheese, shredded
- Salt and black pepper, for tasting

Directions:

1. Preheat outdoor grill to high heat, oil the grate lightly
2. Place pizza dough into a bowl and allow to rise 2-3 times its original size, approx. 1 hour. Flour flat surface area and divide dough in half; roll each section to 10-12 inch diameter circle
3. Place pizza rounds onto a preheated grill, use a wooden paddle and cover; cook until grill marks start to appear at the bottom, approx. 3-5 minutes. Transfer from grill and flip over onto work surface. Low grill temperature to medium.
4. Brush each round with oil. Place half of Asiago cheese onto each crust; add basil, tomatoes and mozzarella cheese. Season with salt and pepper.
5. Transfer pizzas to grill and close the lid. Cook until cheese is melted and bottom rounds produce grill marks, approx. 7-10 minutes. Remove from heat and allow to sit for 5 minutes prior to serving.

Grilled Zucchini
(ready in about 30minutes | Serving 2)

Ingredients:

- 1 large zucchini
- 4 tbsp. butter
- Salt and pepper

Directions:

1. Preheat grill to medium temperature
2. Clean exterior of the zucchini, slice into lengthwise quarters. Place pieces of butter onto each zucchini quarter, season with salt and pepper for flavor. Wrap each quarter in aluminum foil.
3. Place foil wraps onto heated grill and cook for 10-15 minutes on each side.

Smoked Asparagus

(ready in about 1 hour 30 minutes | Serving 1 ½ pounds asparagus)

Ingredients:

- 2 tbsp. of butter
- 4 thinly sliced garlic cloves
- 2 tbsp. lemon juice
- Salt
- ¼ tsp. ground black pepper
- 1 thinly sliced onion
- 1 ½ pounds of trimmed asparagus

Directions:

1. Place charcoal on bottom pan of the smoker. Light coals and allow temperature to rise to 240 degrees F.
2. Melt butter into a small saucepan, stir in garlic and cook over low heat. Remove from heat and combine lemon juice, salt and pepper
3. Place onions into bottom of large cast iron skillet. Spread asparagus over onions. Drizzle garlic mixture and butter over asparagus. Place uncovered skillet (or preferred baking dish) onto the top grate of preheated smoker.
4. Close smoker and cook for 1 hour.

Smoked Herb Chicken

(ready in about 4 hours | Serving 1 chicken)

Ingredients:

- 1 (4 pound) whole chicken
- 3 tbsp. butter
- 1 tbsp. fresh parsley, chopped
- 1 tbsp. fresh oregano, chopped
- 1 tbsp. fresh basil, chopped
- 1 tbsp. fresh chives, finely chopped

Directions:

1. Preheat outdoor grill on low temperature.
2. Rinse chicken inside and out. Pat dry and loosen skin around breast region.
3. Place 3 tbsp. of butter in various regions under the skin. Combine herbs and place half under skin, other half directly inside the chicken.
4. Cook chicken and smoke for 3 hours, juices should run clear once poked with a fork.

Bodacious Barbecue Ribs
(ready in about 17 hours 30 min | Serving 10)

Ingredients:

- 2 tbsp. paprika
- 1 tsp. cayenne pepper
- 1 tsp. garlic powder
- 1 tsp. onion powder
- 1 tbsp. salt
- 1 tsp. ground black pepper
- 2 tsp. ground cumin
- 1 ½ tbsp. brown sugar
- ¼ tsp. ground cinnamon

- 1/8 tsp. ground cloves
- 1/8 tsp. ground nutmeg
- 5 pounds pork spareribs
- 2 pounds hickory soaked wood chips

Directions:

1. Using a medium bowl, stir together paprika, cayenne pepper, onion powder, garlic powder, salt, black pepper, cumin, brown sugar, cloves, cinnamon and nutmeg. Apply well to ribs. Place ribs into large roasting pan, cover and chill overnight. Remove from fridge 1 hour prior to smoking.
2. Prepare outdoor smoker and raise temperature 200-225 degrees F.
3. Smoke ribs for 6-8 hours, replenish woodchips to maintain heat. Ribs should be crispy on the outside and tender inside. Remove from smoker and allow to rest for 20 minutes before serving.

Northern California Smoked Brisket
(ready in about 17 hours 25 minutes | Serving 10-12)

Ingredients:

- 2 dried chilies
- 1 ancho Chile
- 2 dried chipotle chilies
- 2 tbsp. fennel seeds
- 1 tbsp. coriander seeds
- 4-6 black peppercorns
- 1/2 – ¾ cup smoked paprika
- ¼ cup garlic powder

- ¼ cup light brown sugar
- 3 tbsp. kosher salt
- 5 pound flat end piece brisket
- 5 cups Applewood smoking chips, soak in water
- 3 ancho chilies, removed stems
- 2 large white onions, sliced thickly
- 5 garlic cloves
- 1 (28oz.) can of tomatoes
- 2tbsp. red wine vinegar

Directions:

1. To make spice rub; use a large skillet to toast chilies, fennel seeds, peppercorns and coriander seeds on medium-high temperature for approx. 2 minutes. Add to spice grinder and grind well until fine. Use a large mixing bowl to combine spices with remaining rub ingredients.
2. Preheat oven to 300 degrees F
3. Prepare large roasting pan with foil and set to high heat. Put soaked chips on top, place the pan directly over burner, chips should start smoking. Position v-rack over pile of chips and place marinated brisket onto rack. Cover with foil and crimp edges to seal tightly. Reduce temperature to medium and smoke brisket for 15 minutes.
4. Prepare anchos, onion and garlic while brisket is smoking. Remove brisket from roasting pan with rack. Discard chips and foil. Place reserved chilies and vegetables on bottom of pan, place rack with the smoked brisket into roasting pan, so as to sit above the aromatics. Place in middle of oven and roast until brisket becomes tender, approx. 4-4 ½ hours.
5. Transfer brisket from oven to cooling rack. Add pan dripping and vegetables to blender and puree well. Combine red wine vinegar and transfer sauce to serving dish. Slice brisket across the grain and arrange on serving platter or dish, serve with sauce.

Hot Smoked California Yellowtail

(ready in about 2 hour 30 minutes | Serving 6)

Ingredients:

- Fresh yellowtail fish
- Salt water brine

Directions:

1. Pan dress fish for smoking- clean and gut fish, remove tail, head, backbone and pectoral fins. Scale fish and remove bones if desired. Rinse fish to remove traces of blood and remove bruises.
2. Brine fish with adequate ratio of salt and water. During brining, prepare smoker, bring to constant temperature of 200 degrees F.

3. Drain fish and pat dry with paper towels, allow to air dry for half an hour. Lightly oil racks and place fish skin side down.
4. Smoke fish, regulate coals to maintain fire. Cook for approx. 2 hours. Continue to smoke and increase temperature until internal heat of fish reaches 160 degrees F.
5. Serve or wrap and store chilled.

California Avocado-Smoked Corn & Crab Bisque with Avocado-Chive Oil

(ready in about 10 minutes | Serving 55)

Ingredients:

- 8 corn ears, lightly smoked in Applewood for 10-15 minutes
- ½ cup unsalted butter
- 4oz. finely diced white onion
- 1 tsp. smoked paprika

- ½ tsp. pepper
- 2 tbsp. crab base
- 4 cups heavy cream
- 2 cups milk
- 3oz. apple juice
- 3 tsp. turbinado sugar
- 2 fresh avocados; peeled, divided and seeded
- 8oz. claw crab meat
- ½ oz. lime juice
- Salt
- Garnish
- 4 fresh avocados; peeled, divided and seeded
- 5 drops avocado-chive oil
- 8oz. claw crab meat
- 1oz. chives, cut 1 inch length
- Avocado oil
- 1oz. fresh chives, chopped roughly

Directions:

1. Use a mixing bowl, with a box grater to shave smoked kernels off corncobs. Should yield 4 cups of kernels and liquid.
2. Melt butter in large saucepan, add onions and cook on medium temperature until soft, at 7 minutes.
3. Add smoked paprika and black pepper, stir in for 20 seconds and add grated smoked corn + crab base, cook for 2 minutes.
4. Add corncobs, milk, heavy cream, apple juice and turbinado sugar, increase heat to medium-high. Once soup starts simmering, lower heat and allow to simmer for 12 minutes. Remove cobs, use a spatula to scrape excess liquid clinging to them, back into the sauce, discard cobs.
5. Put 2 avocado halves and ½ of soup into blender. Blend on high speed and repeat with remaining avocado + mixture.

6. Add 8oz. of crab meat and lime juice. Bring soup to 140 degrees F. Garnish with diced avocado, chive spears and avocado-chive oil
7. **Avocado Chive Oil**: Heat 5 oz. of avocado oil to 250 degrees F
8. **Place 1 oz**. fresh chives through blender, add hot oil and puree well
9. Strain oil through fine Chinois and cool in ice bath
10. Add salt to taste and mix well.
11. **Assembly:** Divide soup into 1-2oz. portions. Warm the crabmeat.
12. **Garnish each serving with diced avocado, 4-5** drops of avocado oil and 1 tsp. crab meat, along with cut chives.

California Smoked Salmons Sushi Roll
(ready in about 5 hours| Serving 6)

Ingredients:

- 6 tbsps. Rice wine vinegar
- 2 cups Japanese sushi rice
- 1 avacado, peeled, pitted, and sliced
- 6 sheets nori (dry seaweed)

- 8 oz. smoked salmon, cut into strips
- 1 cucumber, peeled and sliced
- 2 tbsps. Wasabi paste

Directions:

1. Drain rice after soaking for 4 hours. Pour 2 cups of water in a rice cooker with the rice (rice will be dry for vinegar later).
2. Mix 6 tbsps. Rice vinegar into the rice immediately after cooking. Spread the rice out on a plate until cooled completely.
3. Lay a bamboo mat out and place seaweed (1 sheet) on the mat. Use the cooled rice to press out a thin layer over the seaweed. Leave both the top and bottom ½ inches of the seaweed uncovered (this will help with sealing). Take wasabi and dot it over the rice. Lay out avocado, cucumber and smoked salmon over the rice leaving 1 inch away from the bottom edge.
4. Wet the edge on top of the seaweed lightly. Start at the bottom and roll to the top using the bamboo mat for help (this will help to make it tight). Repeat this process for the rest of the rolls.

California BBQ Chicken Pizza

(ready in about 50 minutes | Serving 2-9 inch pizzas)

Ingredients:

- 1 tbsp. olive oil
- 10 oz. boneless skinless chicken breasts, cut into ¾ inch cubes
- Pizza dough
- 2 tbsps. Barbecue sauce of your choice
- ½ cup barbecue sauce of your choice
- Cornmeal or semolina or flour
- 2 cups shredded mozzarella cheese
- 2 tbsps. Shredded smoked gouda cheese
- 2 tbsps. Chopped fresh cilantro

- ¼ red onion, sliced into 1/8th inch pieces

Directions:

1. Fry chicken in a large pan with olive oil on medium high heat. When cooked, place it in the refrigerator to chill.
2. Use 2 tbsps. of BBQ sauce to coat the chicken and place the chicken back in the refrigerator.
3. Place the frozen pizza stone in the oven to preheat for 1 hour at 500 °F before cooking.
4. Spread ¼ cup of BBQ sauce over the prepared dough evenly using a large spoon. Take the Gouda cheese and sprinkle 1 tbsp. evenly over the sauce. Sprinkle ¾ cup mozzarella evenly on top. Place half of the chicken evenly covering the cheese. Place 18 to 20 sliced of red onion over the chicken and cheese. Evenly spread the last ¼ cup of Mozzarella over the toppings of the pizza.
5. Place the pizza in the oven, baking until a golden crust is achieved with bubbly cheese in the center. (8 to 10 minutes) Remove from the oven and use 1 tbsp. of cilantro evenly over the surface.

Smoked California Avocado Butter Trout Toast

(ready in about 40 minutes | Serving 1)

Ingredients:

- ½ fresh California avocado, seeded and peeled
- 3 tsp. shallots, very thinly sliced
- ½ tbsp.. lemon juice, divided
- ¼ tbsp.. unsalted butter, room temperature
- ¼ (3.9 oz.) tin oil packed smoked trout, drained
- 1/8th tsp. salt, divided
- ½ tbsp. butter, melted

- 1 slice ¾ inch thick rye bread
- ¼ tbsp. fried capers
- 3 tsp. Italian parsley
- 1 tbsp. lemon zest

Fried Capers
- Capers in brine
- Canola oil, as needed

Directions:

1. Place capers on a paper towel for 30 minutes to dry out.
2. Heat a pot filled with 1 inch of frying oil.
3. Add capers into the hot oil and fry until there are no more bubbles.
4. Remove capers and drain on another paper towel covered plate.
5. Drain the shallots on a paper towel. Set them to the side.
6. Mash the butter, avocado 1/8 tsp. salt and ¼ tbsp. lemon juice blending them until well smoothen.
7. Take the trout and set aside draining the liquid.
8. Slightly toast each side of the bread after brushing with melted butter.
9. Spread the mixture of avocado butter on the toast.
10. Layer the bread first with trout followed by parsley and shallots. Finish topping with remaining lemon juice, capers and garnishing with the lemon zest.

Smoked Tri Tip

(ready in about 1 hours 40 hours | Serving 4 to 6)

Ingredients:

- Coarse salt
- 1 tri tip
- Rub of your choice

Directions:

1. Use coarse salt and BBQ rub of your choice to coat all sides of the tri tip.
2. Preheat the grill to 275 ° with one side not lit.
3. Place wood chips on grayed over coals to smoke.

4. Place the tri tip on the grate of the grill that is not lit to smoke.
5. Smoke until the internal temperature of the tri tip reaches 125 °F (60 to 90 minutes).
6. Move the tri tip over to the direct heat and sear on both sides.
7. Remove from the heat and set to the side to rest for 10 minutes.

California Avocado, Egg and Smoked Salmon Blini
(ready in about 12 minutes | Serving 4)

Ingredients:

- 2 ripe fresh California avocados, quartered, peeled and seeded
- 1 cup crème fraiche
- Salt to taste
- 1 lemon, zested
- 1 tbsp. milk
- 4 eggs
- 16 blinis
- 4 oz. smoked salmon
- Blinis (as needed)
- ½ ripe fresh avocado, cut into thin slices and halved
- 2 ½ tbsp. active dry yeast
- 4 cups milk

- 2 ½ tbsp.. salt
- 3 tbsp. sugar
- 5 large egg yolks
- 5 ¼ cups flour, sifted
- cooking oil spray, (as needed)
- ¾ cup and 2 tbsp. canola or vegetable oil

Directions:

1. Heat yeast, sugar and milk to 110 °F in a small saucepan.
2. Mix flour and salt combining them in a small bowl.
3. Remove the egg yolks and mix them with a whisk into a bowl with oil slowly creating an emulsion.
4. Mix in the flour and milk until fully combined with the egg mixture.
5. Place this batter in a covered large container to proof. The batter needs to proof in a warm place until its size has doubled. This can take 1 to 2 hours.
6. Spray a large skillet on medium heat with cooking oil and pour batter creating 1 ½ inch blinis. Flip them when they begin to bubble. Continue to cook until the sides become golden brown.
7. Mix the avocados, crème fraiche, and lemon zest into a blender. Salt to season to taste. Fill a large resealable plastic bag with the mixture and remove the air before sealing.
8. Mix milk and eggs into a small bowl until well combined. Place a non-stick medium pan on low heat. Pour the egg mixture in the pan making a thin omelet. Place the cooked omelet on a cutting board and use a round cookie cutter to make omelets the size of the blinis.
9. Place an egg round on top of each blini and divide among plates. Place salmon on top of each of these. Take the corner of the bag with the crème fraiche mixture and cut a small hole in it. Squeeze the mixture out on top of each

stacked blini. Use the half of a thin sliced avocado to garnish the top.

California Club Smoked Turkey Quesadilla
(ready in about 10 minutes | Serving 1)

Ingredients:

- Spicy ranch dressing
- Flour tortillas
- Avocado, peeled and chopped
- Smoked turkey, thinly sliced
- Finely shredded Monterey jack cheese
- Roma tomatoes, chopped
- Smoked bacon, cooked and chopped

Directions:

1. Place all the ingredients on a tortilla in layers. Start by placing turkey first and shredded cheese last. Place another tortilla over the top and set in a tortilla cooker.
2. Cook until the tortilla has browned slightly and cheese has melted. Place the tortilla on a cutting board and let stand for 3 to 5 minutes. Cut into wedges using a pizza cutter.

Soupe a l'oignongratinee
(ready in about 3 hours | Serving 8)

Ingredients:

- ¼ cup unsalted butter
- 8 large yellow onions, halved and sliced lengthwise into ¼ inch strips
- 2 2/3 cups water, divided
- Salt
- 5 cups chicken broth
- 2/3 cup dry sherry
- 8 sprigs fresh thyme and one bay leaf tied together
- 2 2/3 cups beef broth
- 2 2/3 cups water (divided)
- 1 loaf French bread
- Fresh ground black pepper
- 1 lb. gruyere, grated

Directions:

1. Preheat your oven at 400 °F. Place butter and onions in a large casserole dish with ¼ tsp. salt, cover and place it in the oven. Stir while cooking every 15 minutes. Continue to cook for about 1 ½ hours or until onions are golden brown and soft.
2. Place the casserole on medium-high heat on the stove and cook until onions become a dark golden brown, stirring frequently.
3. Pour in the first half of water, cooking and stirring constantly for 8 minutes until water has had time to evaporate. Pour in your sherry, cooking it until it has completely evaporated.
4. Stir the second half of water, beef broth and chicken broth along with thyme and gently simmer. Maintain a simmer while reducing the heat and simmering for 40 minutes. Scoop out the thyme and season with salt and pepper to desired taste.
5. Prepare toast while you are simmering the soup. Slice ½ inch sections out of French bread using 1 or 2 slices in a bowl. Crisp the bread until toasted and place it to the side.
6. Spoon 8 soup bowls that are oven proof up to ½ an inch from the rim. Place toast over the soup standing up in the edges. Evenly sprinkle your grated gruyere on the top of the soup. Melt the cheese by placing the bowl under your ovens broiler.

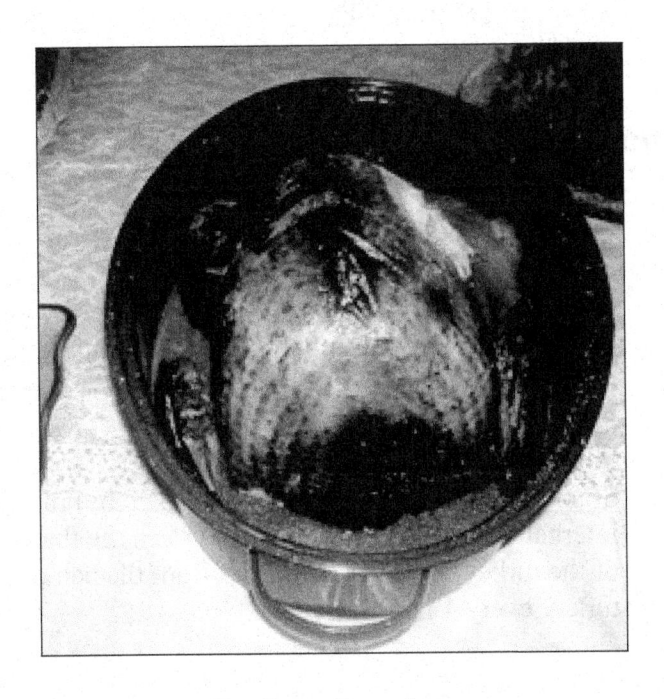

Turkey Smoker
(ready in about 10 + Hours | Serving 1 (10 lb.) Turkey)

Ingredients:

- 4 cloves garlic, crushed
- 1 (10 lb.) Whole Turkey, No neck or giblets
- ½ cup butter
- 2 tbsps. Seasoned salt
- 1 apple, quartered
- 2 (12 fluid oz.) cans cola-flavored carbonated beverage
- 1 tbsp. garlic powder
- 1 onion, quartered

- 1 tbsp. ground black pepper
- 1 tbsp. salt

Directions:

1. Set your smoker to preheat at 230 °F.
2. Place turkey under water to rinse off. Dry the turkey and rub it down with crushed garlic. Use salt to sprinkle the outside. Use a disposable roasting pan to place the turkey in and fill the inside with cola, butter, onion, apple salt, garlic powder, and ground black pepper. Cover the turkey loosely with foil.
3. Smoke the turkey for 10 hours at 230 °F or until the internal temperature becomes 180 °F in the thickest part of the turkey. Pour the drippings from the pan over the turkey every 1 hour.

Grilled Lamb Sausage with Cheese, Tomatoes, and Herbs

(ready in about 30 minutes | Serving 4)

Ingredients:

- 1 tbsp. lemon juice
- 2 tbsps. Sherry vinegar
- 2 tsps. Dijon mustard
- 1 tbsp. shallots, finely diced
- Salt and pepper
- 1 tsp. California clover honey
- 1/3 cup California extra-virgin oil

Salad

- Canola oil
- 1 lb. fresh lamb sausages
- ½ cup black olives, pitted and halved
- Salt and pepper
- ¼ cup pistachios, toasted and chopped
- ¼ cup parsley leaves, roughly chopped
- 6 oz. baby mixed organic greens
- 8 oz. California soft goat cheese, cut into pieces
- 2 tbsps. Basil, chopped
- ½ red onion, thinly sliced
- 2 tbsps. Tarragon, chopped

Directions:

1. To make the vinaigrette you must place lemon juice, vinegar, shallots, honey, and mustard into a small bowl. Season with salt and pepper. Stir the olive oil in slowly.
2. Preheat your grill for cooking directly. Brush canola oil on the sausages and sprinkle with salt and pepper. Cook the sausages through with a golden brown on both sides. Let the sausages stand to the side for 5 minutes.
3. Mix the parsley, olives, cheese, pistachios, onions, greens, tarragon, and basil together. Sprinkle the salad with your vinaigrette and salt and pepper. Serve the salad with the sausage.

California Honey BBQ Sauce

(ready in about 40 minutes | Serving 2 ½ cups)

Ingredients:

- 1 cup water
- 1 cup honey
- 2 tbsps. Worcestershire sauce
- 3 tbsps. cider vinegar
- 1 can (6 oz.) tomato paste
- 2 tbsps. Unsalted butter
- 1 tsp. Dijon mustard
- 1 cup onion, chopped

- 1 ½ tsps.. paprika
- 1 clove garlic, finely chopped.
- ½ tsp. ground black pepper

Directions:

1. Mix all ingredients together in a sauce pan and simmer for about 40 minutes until the sauce thickens.

Southern California Barbecue sauce
(ready in about 1 hour 30 minutes | Serving 12)

Ingredients:

- ¼ cup ketchup
- 2 cups apple cider vinegar
- 1 clove garlic, peeled and minced
- 2 tbsps. Onion, finely chopped
- 1 tsp. chili powder
- 1 tsp. dry mustard
- 1 tsp. cayenne pepper
- 1 tsp. seasoning salt
- 1 cup brown sugar

Directions:
1. In a medium saucepan place bring the apple cider vinegar to a boil. Mix onion, ketchup, dry mustard, garlic, seasoning salt, chili powder, and cayenne pepper. Stir the brown sugar in to the mixture and cook for 10 to 15 minutes, stirring occasionally.
2. Reduce to a simmer stirring occasionally bringing the mixture to a thickened state.

Conclusion

Each state has its own style of cooking and barbecuing. California grilling recipes are delicious and many of them are focused on nutritional based. There are many people who focus their grilling on vegetarian meals and others who focus their attention on meat based meals.

No matter what you choose to eat, vegetarian or meat based meals, we have covered the most delicious recipes that California has to offer. You will love the variations of flavor and texture that we have provided in these 25 unbelievable recipes, followed by two of the most famous California barbecue sauce recipes that will go great on any food.

Enjoy these recipes, and make sure to keep an eye out for the other books in our collection – covering all 50 states in the USA.

*Copyright: Published in the United States by Daniel K. Hinkle/
© Daniel K. Hinkle
All rights Reserved. No part of this publication or the information in it may be quoted from or reproduced in any form by means such as printing, scanning, photocopying or otherwise without prior written permission of the copyright holder.*

Disclaimer and Terms of Use: Effort has been made to ensure that the information in this book is accurate and complete, however, the author and the publisher do not warrant the accuracy of the information, text and graphics contained within the book due to the rapidly changing nature of science, research, known and unknown facts and internet. The Author and the publisher do not hold any responsibility for errors, omissions or contrary interpretation of the subject matter herein. This book is presented solely for motivationaland informational purposes only

Your Free Gift

I wanted to show my appreciation that you support my work so I've put together a free gift for you.

OUTDOOR COOKING ESSENTIALS
Top 25 Camping Food & BBQ Recipes

http://thezenfactory.com/california_texas_free_book/

Just visit the link above to download it now.

I know you will love this gift.

Texas Smoker Recipes: Essential TOP 25 Texas Smoking Meat Recipes

by Daniel Hinkle, Marvin Delgado, Ralph Replogle

Table of Contents

Texas Smoker Recipes: Essential TOP 25 Texas Smoking Meat Recipes 68

by Daniel Hinkle, Marvin Delgado, Ralph Replogle 70

Table of Contents 69

Introduction 73

    Advantages to Smoking Meats Using a Side Box Smoker 74

    Disadvantages 74

The Best Wood for Barbecuing Texas Style 76

Getting Your New Cooker Ready 77

    Preparing Your Smoker 77

    Curing Your Smoker 78

    Your First Cooking Fire 79

Cajun Smoked Beer Chicken 80

    Ingredients: 80

    Directions: 81

Lemon Lime Chicken 82

    Ingredients: 82

    Directions: 82

Smoked Brisket 84

    Ingredients: 84

    Directions: 84

Texas Barbecue Ribs 86

    Ingredients: 86

    Directions: 86

Turkey Times 88
    Ingredients: 88
    Directions: 89
Smoked Chili 90
    Ingredients: 90
    Directions: 91
Coffee Coated Texas Barbecue Brisket 93
    Ingredients: 93
    Directions: 94
Texas Style Barbecue Chicken 95
    Ingredients: 95
    Directions: 96
Filet Mignon with Herb butter and Texas Toast 97
    Ingredients: 97
    Directions: 98
Texas Squealer Burger 99
    Ingredients: 99
    Directions: 99
Texas Backyard Barbecue Chicken Feast 101
    Ingredients: 101
    Directions: 102
Oven Barbecued Chicken Legs 105
    Ingredients: 105
    Directions: 105
Texas Barbecued Mutton 107
    Ingredients: 107
    Directions: 108

Sweet and Sour Pulled Pork Sandwiches 109
    Ingredients: 109
    Directions: 110
Grilled Pork Tenderloin 111
    Ingredients: 111
    Directions: 111
Tomato and Onion Salad 113
    Ingredients: 113
    Directions: 113
Peanutty Coleslaw 115
    Ingredients: 115
    117
Watermelon, Mache and Pecan Salad 117
    Ingredients: 117
    Directions: 117
Bacon Potato Salad 119
    Ingredients: 119
    Directions: 119
Barbecue Coleslaw 121
    Ingredients: 121
    Directions: 122
Texan Pecan Pie 123
    Ingredients: 123
    Directions: 123
Texas Brownies 125
    Ingredients: 125
    Directions: 126

Apple Cake with Cream Cheese 127
    Ingredients: 127
    Directions: 128
Old Fashion Texas Cherry Dumplings 129
    Ingredients: 129
    Directions: 129
Tasty Fruit Cobbler 131
    Ingredients: 131
    Directions: 131
County Line Bourbon Sauce 133
    Ingredients: 133
    Directions: 133
Texas Chainsaw Barbecue Sauce 135
    Ingredients: 135
    Directions: 136
Conclusion 135

Introduction

The most important aspect of smoking and grilling is choosing the right grill for your type of cooking. Each type of pit provides a different type and time of cooking, so it is important to choose a pit that accommodates your specific style.

One of the best pits you can find to barbecue Texas Style has an offset firebox that is separate from the cooking chamber. This allows you to have a barbecue experience that is thorough, but fits almost any budget. Since the firebox is not located right below the food, it allows you to cook your food at a consent temperature, but allows the smoke to reach the meat in a method that properly heats the food and cooks it evenly.

While there are many cookers on the market, we do not recommend using a vertical smoker. These types of smokers cause the fire to be right under the meat which allows too much direct heat, charring the outside while leaving the inside raw. It can also make your meat very tough instead of tender and juicy.

The most common type of smoker for Texas Barbecue can be purchased at Lowes and is called the Oklahoma Joe. It provides the previously mentioned offset firebox, a cooking area that will accommodate 2 briskets, air vents that are adjustable, and a thermometer that allows you to monitor the cooking temperature inside the cooker's chamber. It is recommended to install the grommet and thermometer before you try to cook because it prevents the meat from scorching or being undercooked. The ideal temperature to keep your meat at is right below 250 degrees F.

Using a smoker that is too small can cause your meat to be over-smoked. If you have a smaller cooker, wrap your meat in aluminum foil for the first half of the cooking process. Make sure to rotate your meat halfway through the cooking process as well. This will prevent uneven cooking due to the offset box.

While it is possible to use charcoal to smoke your meat, it is geared more toward grilling. It is recommended that you use a mix of different woods that are recommended for smoking.

Advantages to Smoking Meats Using a Side Box Smoker

- The boxes are inexpensive and available at hardware stores and online

- All of the advantages of a pro-grill are included, it is just smaller

- You can create amazing barbecue, especially Texas Style

Disadvantages

- The fire being close to the cooking chamber can cause normal cooking temperatures and throw off normal cookingtemperatures

- The meat does not always cook evenly, therefore it must be turned

- There is no way to add in water, to add humidity

- Your meat will receive direct smoke and could need to be covered through part of the cooking process to avoid burning

The Best Wood for Barbecuing Texas Style

When you think of Texas barbecue, you may wonder what the best style wood for smoking the perfect brisket is. The truth is that the ideal wood for smoking and grilling Texas style is Mesquite. The wood is well known throughout Texas and over half of the state is covered with Mesquite wood.

The mesquite tree is a small shrub. It is hard to believe that such a small shrub can create such a delicious flavor when smoked but it is the only way to create the perfect Texas style barbecue or smoked meat.

Mesquite wood burns hot and creates a lot of smoke. It is excellent for larger cuts of meat and creates a distinct, sweet, smoky flavor that most woods cannot manage. If you don't live near the southwest, it can be expensive to purchase this wood, but it burns for a long time so it is worth the expense that you go through.

The advantage to using mesquite wood is that it is excellent for cooking a wide majority of meats that are smoked or grilled, including:

- Brisket
- Ribeye
- Whole chickens
- Steaks
- Hamburgers
- And more….

Mesquite wood also mixes well with other woods, including apple, maple, cedar and more.

Getting Your New Cooker Ready

When you get a new cooker, you cannot simply throw the meat in with some wood and hope that it turns out tasting great. There are some things you must do to ensure that your cooker is ready to smoke meat.

Preparing Your Smoker

After you have unpacked and assembled your new smoker, make sure that you have added the proper grates to the firebox to protect the bottom. This is the area of your new grill that reaches extremely high temperatures and cooking the wood directly on the bottom of the fire box will cause the box to weaken and break over time.

You can eventually expect some bubbling in the factory pain in this area and you will notice that the paint will begin to peel. It is recommended to regularly retouch your grill with high heat black pain and keep it covered when it isn't in use. This will prevent rust.

Ensure that you make note of the location of each air vent. These are necessary to adjusting the temperature of the fire and you will use them to control the heat when you are barbecuing and smoking your meats.

Curing Your Smoker

If you want your fir pit to last, you must cure the smoker before using it. Meat absorbs flavor from the cooker and if you have fresh steel with the oils used from manufacturing, your meat will taste like these contaminants.

In order to cure your fire pit, start a fire as though you were going to cook on it. Allow the cooking areas to reach 400 degrees F. Once you reach this temperature, you will want to reduce the heat to 250 degrees F and allow it to smoke for several hours. This allows any contaminants to burn off while creating the recommended layer of creole, or burnt sap. The old saying, the more you smoke on a pit the better your food tastes is definitely true. So the thicker the layer of burnt material you have in your cooker, the better it is to cook on.

Your First Cooking Fire

Arrange logs in a manner where the air can get around each log evenly. Start with smaller logs and then move to bigger logs as the fire heats up. The first fire should be fairly large, as it will help burn down the coals before you start cooking.

One of the best methods of starting the fire is using a propane torch. If you do not have a propane torch, use a small pile of charcoal soaked in lighter fluid under your logs to get it going.

Open all of the air vents so that the fire gets the maximum amount of air. Light your fire and allow it to burn until you have a good deal of coals that are self-sustaining. Typically, this takes approximately 20 to 30 minutes depending on how green the wood is. When you are warming up your fire, you should reach temperatures of close to 400 degrees F.

Once your box has reached the temperature of 400 degrees F. Shut down the air vents in order to extinguish your flames for a few minutes. Open the air vents so that the fire goes into a smoldering state. You do not want the fire to go completely out, just bring it to a shouldering state.

Cajun Smoked Beer Chicken

(ready in about 4 hours 30 minutes | Servings 4 to 6)

Ingredients:

- 3 to 4 lb. Chicken
- ½ onion, chopped
- 3 cloves garlic
- Beer of your choice

Injection Ingredients
- 2 tbsps. Tony Chachere's seasoning
- ½ cup melted butter
- 1 tsp. garlic powder

Rub Ingredients
- Tony Chachere's seasoning

- Olive oil

Mop Ingredients
- ½ cup olive oil
- Spray bottle
- 1 cup of apple cider

Directions:

1. Mix all the ingredients for the injection in a bowl and whisk well.
2. Use an injector and evenly distribute the injection to all parts of the chicken.
3. Use the olive oil to rub down the chicken and rub the now oiled chicken with the seasoning rub.
4. Take the beer and drink the first half of it. Widen the top and place your onion and garlic inside.
5. Sit the bird upright placing the can inside the chicken.
6. Get your smoker preheated to 250 °F and use hickory wood chips to smoke with.
7. Use the ingredients for the mop mixture and mix them in a spray bottle by shaking them.
8. Place your beer filled chicken on the smoker spraying it down with the mop spray. Continue to spray every 30 minutes keeping it moist.
9. Cook the chicken for 3 to 4 hours or until internal temperatures meet 175 °F

Lemon Lime Chicken

(ready in about 4 hour 30 min | Serving 4-6)

Ingredients:

- 4 cups Lemon-lime tequila mix
- 1 (5 lb.) Whole chicken
- 1 tbsp. onion powder
- 1 tbsp. garlic powder
- 1 tbsp. cayenne lemon pepper

Directions:
1. Combine tequila mix and seasonings in a large reseal able plastic bag with the whole chicken. Seal the bagged chicken and place it in the refrigerator to marinade for 6 hours.
2. Preheat your smoker to 250 °F

3. Remove the chicken from the refrigerator and remove it from the bad. Place it on the preheated grill.
4. Lightly coat the chicken with lemon pepper.
5. Smoke the chicken for 4 hours adding a handful of wood chips every half hour until internal temperatures reach at least 175 °F.

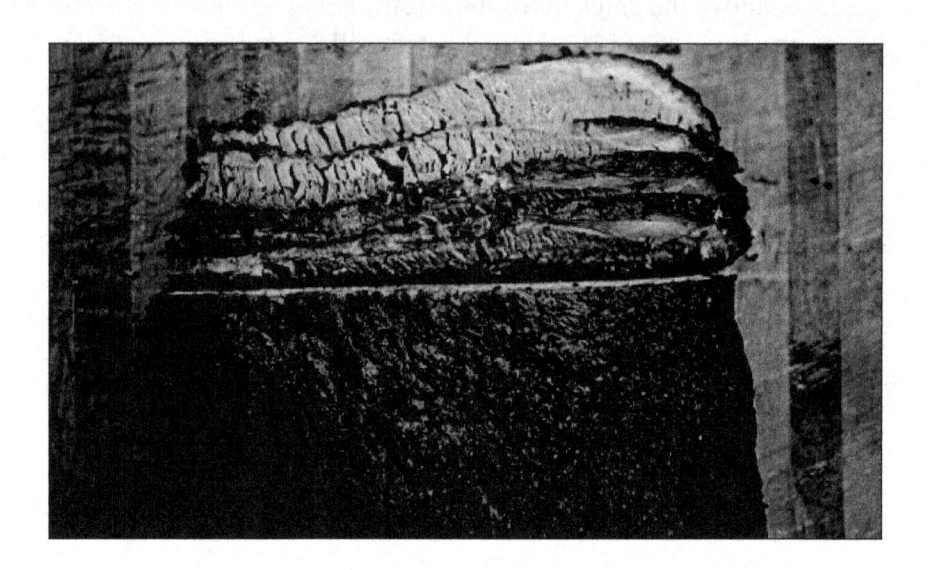

Smoked Brisket

(ready in about 6 hours | Servings 8 to 10)

Ingredients:

- 1 – 12 pound beef brisket, fat trimmed down to ¼ inch thickness
- 1/3 cup salt
- 1/3 cup ground black pepper

Directions:

1. Mix salt and pepper in a small bowl. Season the meat while it is still wet so that the seasoning sticks to the meat well.

2. Allow the meat to sit for at least 1 hour at room temperature so that the seasoning has time to flavor the meat.

Prepare Grill
3. Fill the smoker with charcoal. Allow to burn for approximately 10 to 15 minutes or until the coals are covered with a thin layer of ash.
4. Pour the charcoal into one side of the grill. Place three chunks of wood next to the coals. This will allow the wood to catch slowly and smolder.
5. Check the coals every 45 minutes and add to the fire when your grill can no longer maintain a temperature of 250 degrees F.
6. It should not take more than 4 to 6 chimneyfuls of coals to cook the brisket.
7. Flip the brisket and rotate it every three hours. When it is finished cooking, the meat should be tender, but not falling apart. A meat thermometer inserted into the thickest portion of the meat should read between 195 degrees F – 205 degrees F, which should take 10 to 12 hours.

Texas Barbecue Ribs

(ready in about 6 hours 30 minutes| Servings 4)

Ingredients:

- Honey
- Brown sugar
- 11 oz. chili powder
- 1/3 cup brown sugar
- 2 tbsps. Garlic powder
- 2 tbsps. Seasoning salt
- 2 tbsps. Cayenne
- 2 tbsps. Onion powder
- 2 tbsps. Paprika
- 1 tbsp. cracked black pepper

Directions:

1. Preheat your smoker to 250 °F using hickory or pecan woodchips, which had been soaked in water.
2. Rub your ribs down with your dry rub made of the ingredients and allow to sit for one hour.
3. Place the ribs on indirect heat for 2 ½ hours.
4. Place the ribs in some foil and cover with honey and brown sugar.
5. Cook for 2 ½ to 3 hours longer and rib bones pull out easily.

Turkey Times
(ready in about 7 hours | Servings 8 to 10)

Ingredients:

- Salt, to taste
- Red pepper flakes, to lightly coat
- 4 cloves garlic, smashed
- 2 jalapeno peppers, sliced
- 13 to 15 pound turkey
- 1 tbsp. chili powder
- 1 tbsp. ground coriander
- 2 tsp. ground cumin
- 1 tsp packed brown sugar, dark brown
- 1 tsp. garlic powder
- 1 tsp rosemary, fresh and chopped
- 1 tsp chopped thyme, fresh
- Ground black pepper, to taste
- 2 tbsp. mayonnaise
- 1 pound sliced bacon, preferably applewood smoked

Directions:

1. Create brine by combining the 1 cup salt, pepper flakes, garlic, jalapenos and 2 quarts hot water in a large pot. Stir the mixture until the salt is dissolved. Place the turkey in the mixture breast side down. Add enough cold water to fully submerge the turkey. Cover the pot and refrigerate for 12 hours. Drain the turkey, rinse and pat dry.
2. Soak 2 large bags of mesquite and 2 large bags of Applewood in water for 1 hour.
3. Create spice blend by combining chili powder, coriander, cumin brown sugar, garlic powder, rosemary, thyme 1 tbsp. salt, and 2 tsp pepper. Loosen the skin of the turkey with your fingers gently. Rub the meat with mayonnaise.
4. Rub the spice blend all over the skin of the bird. Put the turkey in a large roasting pan breast side up.
5. Lay ¾ of the bacon over the breast of the bird overlapping slices and securing with toothpicks.
6. Wrap the legs with the remaining portion of the bacon, secure it with toothpicks.
7. Drain the water from the woodchips and prepare the smoker per manufacturer's directions. Preheat smoker box to 210 degrees F. Put turkey, still in the disposable pan, on the smoker grates. Cover and cook for 6 to 7 hours, or until a meat thermometer registers 190 degrees in the thickest portion of the turkey.
8. Make sure to add a few handfuls of soaked wood chips every hour to maintain the required level of smoke. If the bacon is browning too quickly, cover the turkey loosely with foil.
9. Allow to rest for 30 minutes before removing bacon and carving. Chop up the bacon and sprinkle it on top of the carved turkey.

Smoked Chili

(ready in about 4 hours 30 min | Serving 6)

Ingredients:

- 5 pounds ground beef
- 2 tbsp. canola oil
- 1 large onion, chopped
- 1 tbsp. garlic, minced
- 2 heaping tbsp. all-purpose flour
- 28 ounce can diced tomatoes
- 2 six ounce cans tomato paste
- 4 ounces of aged cheese
- 2 tbsp. brown sugar
- 1 tsp ground cinnamon
- 2 beef bouillon cubes
- ½ tsp cayenne powder

- SYD Hot rub, to taste
- Chili spice dunk
- 3 heaping tbsp. mild chili powder
- 2 heaping tbsp. paprika
- 2 tbsp. ground cumin

Directions:

1. Sauté the ground beef in large sauce pan with a little canola oil until the beef. Season with SYD hot rub to taste. Transfer the beef to a cast iron pot with a slotted spoon to prevent too much grease transfer.
2. Drain off any fat that did make it to the pot leaving only 4 tbsp. of fat in the previous pan. Add in onions and sauté until they are translucent. Add in chopped garlic and cook for a few more minutes. Use a slotted spoon to transfer the onion and garlic mixture to the pot you are cooking the chili in.
3. Whisk in two tbsp. of flour to the oil under a medium-low heat to make a roux. Add a little more oil if needed to create the right consistency. The result should feel like uncooked pancake batter and should be light brown.
4. Once the roux is light brown, turn the heat up and add ½ cup of water at a time. To whisk the roux into gravy. Once you have reached the consistency of gravy, stop adding water.
5. Add in the canned tomatoes, tomato paste, block of cheese, brown sugar, cinnamon, crumbled bouillon cubes, cayenne, salt and pepper. Pour the entire amount Pour the entire mixture into the pan you cooked your ground beef. If you're not going to smoke your chili on the pit, you can transfer the chili to a crockpot or stove pot to simmer.
6. Add half of the spice dunk mixture and mix thoroughly. Place the pot on the pit at 250 to 300 degrees F. Smoke the chili uncovered for several

hours. Stir the chili every hour and add more water as needed.
7. Add the remaining ½ of the spice dunk mixture 15 minutes before you plan to eat the chili. Taste the chili before serving and adjust spices.

Coffee Coated Texas Barbecue Brisket

(ready in about 7 hours | Serving 18)

Ingredients:

- 6 cups oak or hickory wood chips
- 1 tbsp. ground coffee
- 1 tbsp. kosher salt
- 1 tbsp. dark brown sugar
- 2 tsp. paprika
- 2 tspanchoChile powder
- 1 tsp garlic powder
- 1 tsp onion powder
- 1 tsp ground cumin

- 1 tsp freshly ground black pepper
- 1 brisket that weighs 4 ½ to 5 pounds, about 3 inches thick.

Directions:

1. Soak the woodchips in water for at least 1 hour, drain completely.
2. Combine the coffee and following 8 ingredients in a bowl. Pat the brisket dry and rub with mixture.
3. Remove the grill rack and set aside, prepare for indirect grilling. This means that you will be heating one side to high and the other side will not have any heat. Use a knife and pierce the bottom of a disposable pan several times. Place this pan on the heated side of the grill. Add 1 ½ cups wood chips to the pan. Place a second disposable pan on the unheated side of the grill. Pour 2 cups of water in the pan. Allow to sit for 15 minutes or until the woodchips are smoking. Reduce the heat to medium low and maintain a temperature around 225 degrees F.
4. Place the grill rack on the grill and place the brisket in a small roasting pan. Place it on the unheated side of the grill rack. Close the lid and allow to cook for 6 hours, or until the meat thermometer reaches 195 degrees F in the thickest portion of the meat.
5. Ensure that you add fresh wood chips after 4 hours. Cover the pan with foil for the last 2 hours. Remove from the grill and allow to stand for 30 minutes, still covered.
6. Unwrap the brisket, reserving juices. Trim the fat from the brisket and use a large zip-top plastic bag inside of a 4 cup glass measuring cup. Pour juices through a sieve into a bag. Discard solids. Allow drippings to stand for 10 minutes. Seal the bag. Cut off one corner of the bag and allow the drippings to drain into a bowl. Before the fat reaches the opening, stop the flow. Discard fat. Cut the brisket across the grain into thin slices. Serve with the juices.

Texas Style Barbecue Chicken
(ready in about 50 minutes | Serving 8)

Ingredients:

- 8 boneless breast halves
- 3 tbsp. brown sugar
- 1 tbsp. ground paprika
- 1 tsp salt
- 1 tsp dry mustard
- ½ tsp chili powder
- ¼ c distilled white vinegar
- 1/8 tsp cayenne pepper
- 2 tbsp. Worcestershire sauce
- ½ cup tomato – vegetable juice cocktail
- ½ c ketchup
- ¼ c water
- 2 cloves garlic, minced

Directions:

1. Preheat oven to 350 degrees F.
2. Place chicken breasts in a single layer in a 9 x 13 inch baking dish.
3. In a medium bowl, mix together the brown sugar, paprika, salt, dry mustard, chili powder, vinegar, cayenne pepper, Worcestershire sauce, vegetable juice cocktail, ketchup, water and garlic. Pour sauce over the chicken breasts.
4. Bake uncovered for 35 minutes in the oven. Remove the chicken breasts, shred with a fork and put back in sauce. Bake for an additional 10 minutes so that the chicken can soak up more flavor. Serve on a bed of rice with freshly ground pepper

Filet Mignon with Herb butter and Texas Toast
(ready in about 45 min | Serving 4)

Ingredients:

- 1 tbsp. butter, softened
- 3 tsp extra-virgin olive oil, divided
- 1 tbsp. minced fresh chives
- 1 tbsp. capers, rinsed and chopped
- 3 tsp minced fresh marjoram, divided
- 1 tsp lemon juice
- ¾ tsp salt, divided
- 1 tbsp. minced rosemary
- 2 cloves garlic (1 minced, 1 peeled and halved)

- 1 pound filet mignon, bout 1 ½ inches thick, trimmed and cut into 4 pieces.
- 4 slices bread of your choice
- 4 cups watercress, trimmed and chopped

Directions:

1. Preheat a grill to high.
2. Mash butter in a small bowl with the back of a spoon until it is soft and creamy. Stir in 2 teaspoons oil until it is combined. Add chives, capers, 1 tsp marjoram, ½ tsplemon zest, lemon juice, ½tsp salt and ¼ tsp pepper. Cover and place in the freezer to chill.
3. Combine the following in a medium bowl: 1 tsp oil, 2 tsp marjoram, ½ tsp lemon zest, ¼ tsp salt and pepper, rosemary, and minced garlic. Rub on both sides of the bread with the halved clove of garlic. Discard garlic.
4. Grill the steak for 5 minutes per side for a medium rare doneness. Grill the bread until lightly toasted, 30 seconds to 1 minute per side.
5. Place one piece of toast n each serving plate. Top with watercress and top with steak.
6. Spread the herb butter on top of the steaks and let rest for 5 minutes before cutting or serving.

Texas Squealer Burger

(ready in about 50 minutes | Serving 6 to 8)

Ingredients:

- 1 ½ pounds ground beef
- 12 slices flavored bacon, uncooked
- 1 ½ tbsp. grill seasoning
- 1 tsp garlic powder
- 1 tbsp. minced dried onion
- ¼ c Worcestershire sauce
- Salt and pepper to taste

Directions:

1. Chop bacon finely with a sharp knife. Slice it in half and then into strips. Dice the bacon finely.

2. Mix all ingredients in a large bowl and add bacon to the mixture.
3. Form patties and put them in the freezer for 30 minutes before grilling.
4. Grill patties for about 5 minutes on each side. Allow them to rest for 5 minutes before cutting or serving.
5. Top burgers with cheese and your favorite toppings.

Texas Backyard Barbecue Chicken Feast
(ready in about 1 hour 15minutes | Serving 4)

Ingredients:

- 1 whole chicken, cut into quarters
- 1 tbsp. vegetable oil
- Salt
- Pepper
- Dried thyme, to taste
- Crushed red bell pepper flakes, to taste
- 3 cups barbecue sauce
- Country greens cornbread, pan stuffing, recipe included
- Peach – Jalapeno Chutney, recipe included

Country Greens-Cornbread Pan Stuffing
- 4 pounds fresh collard greens
- 1 smoked ham hock
- 8 cup chicken stock, plus 2 to 3 cups more, if needed
- 1 large onion, peeled but kept whole
- 2 dried red chilies
- 1 tsp cracked black pepper
- Salt
- Pepper vinegar

For the Cornbread
- 1 cup yellow cornmeal
- 1 cup all-purpose flour
- ¼ cup sugar
- 4 tsp baking powder
- ½ tsp salt
- 1 cup milk
- 2 extra-large eggs, lightly beaten
- ¼ cup unsalted butter, melted

Peach – Jalapeno Chutney:
- 5 ripe peaches
- 1 tbsp. diced ginger
- 1 tbsp. sugar
- 1 tsp ground cinnamon
- 2 tsp lemon juice

Directions:

1. Make sure that the whole chicken is rinsed under cold running water. Quarter the chicken and brush with vegetable oil. Season with salt, pepper, thyme and pepper flakes on both sides. Allow them to set for a while for the seasoning to sink in.

2. Clean the grill and ensure that all ashes are discarded. Grates must be brushed clean. Add your wood or charcoal and ignite. When the charcoal has burned to the point where it is covered with a thin layer of white ash, add in the chicken quarters. Make sure that the skin side is facing downward so that the fat can render from the skin. Do not allow the skin side to remain facing down for a long duration of time because this can cause the grill to flare up, resulting in burnt skin. Make sure to pay careful attention to what the grill is doing at all times.
3. Add in hickory soaked chips to the edge of the fire, one handful at a time. This will start the smoking process. Close the lid or place the top back on the grill. The skin will take approximately 10 minutes to render completely.
4. When the smoke begins to die down, add in another handful of hickory chips.
5. Grill the chicken for another 15 minutes and make sure that the meat is cooking evenly on both sides if one side is cooking faster than the other, allow that side more time facing downward on the grill.
6. Begin basting each piece of chicken with barbecue sauce. Turn each piece to prevent burning.
7. Remove chicken from the grill onto a platter and cover with aluminum foil until you are ready to serve them.

Greens

1. Pick through the pile of greens and throw away any that have large stems or have brown or yellow discoloration on the leaves. Was the greens thoroughly to remove any grit. Cut greens into bite sized pieces.
2. Place the ham hock, onion, chiles, and pepper in a large pot over medium-high heat. Add enough stock to cover them with 1 inch of liquid. Bring to a boil. Reduce the heat to medium-low and simmer for 40 to 60 minutes. The cooking time will depend greatly on the age of the greens. The liquid should reduce by ¾

during cooking time. Remove the ham hock and pull the meat from the bones. Cut the meat into a medium sized dice and put it back in with the greens. Remove the onion, chop finely and place back in the greens. Season with pepper vinegar.

3. Remove from pan and place in a bowl covered with foil while you finish the cornbread.

Cornbread

1. Preheat the oven to 425 degrees F.

2. Grease a 10 inch cast iron skillet and place in the oven.

3. Combine ingredients and pour batter into the hot pan. Place the pan back in the oven and bake for 20 to 25 minutes. The edges should be light brown and the bread should be firm. Remove from the oven and allow to cool. Cut the cornbread into 1 inch dice.

Peach-Jalapeno Chutney

1. Peel and pit all peaches. Dice three peaches into medium dice. Add to a sauce pan ginger, sugar, cinnamon and lemon juice. Bring the mixture to a boil in a medium sauce pan. Stir until the mixture is thick and hot. Cook for about 5 to 6 minutes. Pour peaches into a sauce pan and cook for about 4 minutes, or until the mixture is thick and hot. Set aside.

Oven Barbecued Chicken Legs

(ready in about 1 hour 15 minutes | Serving 3)

Ingredients:

- 6 chicken drumsticks
- ½ c water
- 1/3 c ketchup
- 1/3 c white vinegar
- ¼ c light brown sugar
- 4 tbsp. butter
- 2 tsp Worcestershire sauce
- 2 tsp. dry mustard
- 2 tsp chili powder, or to taste

Directions:

1. Preheat oven to 400 degrees F.

2. Place drumsticks in a disposable baking pan or a baking dish.
3. Whisk together water, vinegar, ketchup, butter, Worcestershire sauce, mustard, salt, and chili powder. Pour the mixture over drumsticks. Cover the pan with foil and allow to cook for about 1 hour, or until the juices run clear. Make sure to turn the chicken ½ way through. You will know the chicken is done when you insert a meat thermometer into the chicken, near the bone and it reads 165 degrees F.

Texas Barbecued Mutton

(ready in about 3 ½ hours | Serving 6)

Ingredients:

- 1 square cut lamb shoulder roast, 7 to 8 pounds
- 1 tbsp. Kosher salt
- 1 tbsp. course ground black pepper
- 1 tsp. dried thyme

For Broth
- 2 tbsp. olive oil
- 2 celery stalks, cleaned and chopped
- 1 onion, chopped
- 4 cloves garlic, minced
- 14.5 ounce can tomatoes, stewed
- 2 carrots, peeled and chopped into circles ½ inch thick
- 1 serranochilies, stemmed, seeded and cut in half.

- The leaves from 3 sprigs of fresh rosemary, cleaned and chopped
- The leaves from 3 sprigs fresh thyme, cleaned and chopped
- Salt and pepper, to taste

For Serving
- Mustard barbecue sauce

Directions:

1. Rinse the meat and pat dry. Combine salt, pepper and thyme. Rub the meat with the seasoning mixture and allow to sit for an hour. Light 25 charcoal briquettes in chimney and prepare the grill with coals place onto one side. Over a hot fire, brown lamb for 10-15 minutes, turning regularly until browned. Transfer to cool side of grill, place hardwood chips/chunks onto coals and close the lid. For 3 hours, allow roast to smoke at approx. 250 degrees F, turning evenly.
2. Over medium heat, heat oil in a soup pot. Add celery and onions. Cook and stir for five minutes until softened, throw in garlic and cook for a few more minutes. Add in remaining vegetables, herbs and 8 cups of water, bring everything to boil. Reduce heat and allow to simmer.
3. Put in more wood and charcoal to fire. Place metal roasting pan on a grill, right over the coals. Pour broth into the roasting pan, place meat into the roasting pan with soup. Let the meat smoke and simmer for one hour (more if needed), replenish liquid levels if required.
4. Using pot holders or fire gloves, remove pan from fire and cover roast, including roasting pan, with aluminum foil and tightly seal. Return to fire. Simmer over coals for another hour, meat should be tender with shape intact.
5. Reserve the broth and remove meat from bone. Serve meat with bread, mustard barbecue sauce and broth

Sweet and Sour Pulled Pork Sandwiches

(ready in about 2 hours 50 minutes | Serving 2 ½ dozen)

Ingredients:

- 1 Tablespoon of Canola Oil
- 4 pounds of Pork Shoulder Roast
- 1 Cup of B.B.Q Sauce
- 1 ½ Cups of Apple Sauce mixed with a tablespoon of Balsamic Vinegar.
- ½ Cup of Vegetable Broth

(Of course you can purchase vegetable broth at your local grocery store however, if you are in the habit of steaming your vegetables as it is, the best and most healthy vegetable broth comes by freezing your stock and making your own vegetable broth.)

- 1 1/2 cups of honey or 1 cup of Beehive
- 1 teaspoon of cayenne pepper
- 1 Large Yellow Onion minced very finely. Add five or
- Six shallots. These also must be chopped very finely.
- Even maybe run though the blender for quick time.
- Add a pinch or two of Garlic Powder a
- Tablespoon of Basil. Before mixing these ingredients
- in a separate mixing bowl, you may opt to add a little
- Dill. I like it, but it may not be for everyone.
- 8 Kaiser Buns
- 2-4 Tablespoons of Garlic Butter

Directions:

1. Before anything you take your vegetable oil and pour it into the slow cooker. Once you've done that, then add the actual pork roast in with it. Let it sit for about two minutes before pouring in your barbecue sauce, then your apple sauce/balsamic vinegar, and vegetable broth. Once those ingredients are added, slowly start to stir in the honey, mustard, cayenne pepper, and your spiced onion/shallots. Cover and cook on high for anywhere between 5-6 hours. You will know it's done when you can stick a fork in it and it easily shreds.
2. After removing the pork for. The slow cooker and shredding it with what's commonly don't with a couple of forks, put the pork back into the slow cooker so it is able to marinate in its own delicious juices
3. The very last thing to do is to make some delicious, crispy, garlic buttery Kaiser buns for your sandwich. Lather each side with the garlic butter you prepared earlier. After toasting the laser buns, scoop the pork into them and enjoy!!

Grilled Pork Tenderloin
(ready in about 55 minutes | Serving 6)

Ingredients:

- 1 pound of pork tenderloins
- 1 tsp garlic powder
- 1 tsp salt
- 1 tsp ground black pepper
- 1 cup barbecue sauce

Directions:

1. Prepare the grill for indirect placement of heat
2. Season the meat with salt, pepper and garlic powder

3. Lightly oil grate. Place tenderloin on the grate, place drip pan under meat. Cook over the indirect heat for approx. 30 minutes
4. With barbecue sauce, brush sauce on tenderloin meat. Cook for a further 15 minutes, temperature should read 145 degrees F in the center. Allow pork to rest for 10 minutes. Slice and serve with extra barbecue sauce, for dipping.

Tomato and Onion Salad

(ready in about 2 hours 10 minutes | Serving 8)

Ingredients:

- ¼ cup extra virgin olive oil
- 1 ½ tbsp. balsamic vinegar
- ½ tsp salt
- ¼ tsp sugar
- ¼ tsp pepper
- 4 tomatoes, large, sliced thinly
- 1 sweet onion, medium-sized, sliced thinly
- ¼ cup fresh basil, chopped

Directions:

1. In a large bowl, whisk together first 5 ingredients. Arrange onion and tomato slices in rows, using a serving dish. Garnish with fresh basil and evenly drizzle with marinade. Cover and allow to stand for 2 hours. Serve with slotted spoon.

Peanutty Coleslaw

(ready in about 1 hour 15 minutes | Serving 6)

Ingredients:

- 1/2 cup fresh cilantro chopped
- ¼ cup green onions, chopped
- 3 tbsp white vinegar
- 1 tbsp sesame oil
- 2 tbsp mayo
- 1 tsp sugar
- 1 tsp fresh ginger, grated
- 2 tsp wasabi paste
- ½ tsp salt
- ½ tsp pepper
- 1 (16oz) package of shredded coleslaw mix
- ¾ cup lightly salted peanuts

1. Combine first 10 ingredients in a large bowl, using a whisk. Add in coleslaw mix and stir well. Cover and refrigerate for 1 hour, stir in peanuts prior to servin

Watermelon, Mache and Pecan Salad

(ready in about 45 minutes | Serving 6-8)

Ingredients:

- ¾ cup pecans, chopped
- 5 cup watermelon, cubed and seeded
- 1 (6oz) package of mache, washed thoroughly
- Pepper jelly vinaigrette
- 1 cup Gorgonzola cheese, crumbled

Directions:

1. Preheat oven to 350 degrees F. Arrange pecans into a single layer, among a baking sheet. Bake for 5-7 minutes

until fragrant and lightly roasted. Cool for 15 minutes on wiring rack.
2. Combine mache and watermelon into a large bowl. Add vinaigrette, toss gently to coat. Transfer watermelon mixture to serving dish and sprinkle with cheese and pecans.

Bacon Potato Salad

(ready in about 1 hour 33 minutes | Serving 6)

Ingredients:

- 6 chopped green onions
- 2 finely chopped celery ribs
- 2 tbsp diced pimiento, drained
- 3/4 tsp salt
- ¼ tsp pepper
- ½ cup mayo
- ½ cup sour cream
- Garnishes: paprika, celery sticks

Directions:

1. In boiling water, cook potatoes and cover in a Dutch oven over medium heat, cook for 15-18 minutes. Drain and allow to cool slightly.
2. Transfer potatoes to a large bowl. Add green onions, bacon, celery ribs, pimiento, salt and pepper. Combine mayo and sour cream together in a separate container, blend well and pour over potato mixture, toss gently to coat. Cover and chill for 1 hour. Garnish (if desired) and serve.

Barbecue Coleslaw

(ready in about 2 hours 20 minutes | Serving 8-10)

Ingredients:

- 2 (10oz) packages of finely shredded cabbage
- 1 shredded carrot
- ½ cup sugar
- ½ tsp salt
- 1/8 tsp pepper
- ½ cup mayo
- ¼ cup buttermilk
- 2 ½ tbsp lemon juice
- 1 ½ tbsp. white vinegar

Directions:

1. Combine carrot and cabbage together in large bowl
2. Combine and whisk sugar, along with remaining ingredients. Blend well and toss with vegetables. Cover and chill for 2 hours.

Texan Pecan Pie

(ready in about 1 hour | Serving 6)

Ingredients:

- 3 eggs
- 1 tsp vanilla
- 1/3 cup sweet butter, melted
- Pinch of salt
- 1 cup dark brown sugar
- 1-1 ½ cup pecan halves
- 1 cup white corn syrup
- 1 (9 inch) pie shell, unbaked

Directions:

1. In a large bowl, combine all ingredients except for pie shell. Mix well and pour into 9 inch pie shell.
2. Place into oven and bake at 350 degrees F for 45-50 minutes. Serve with ice cream, if desired

Texas Brownies

(ready in about 20 minutes | Serving 5)

Ingredients:

- 2 cup all-purpose flour
- 2 cup granulated sugar
- ½ cup butter
- ½ cup shortening
- 1 cup strong brewed coffee (or water)
- ¼ cup dark cocoa, unsweetened
- ½ cup buttermilk
- 2 eggs
- 1 tsp baking soda
- 1 tsp vanilla
- 1 (17 ½ x 11 inch) jelly roll pan
- **For Frosting**
- ½ cup butter

- 4 tbsp. cocoa
- 6 tbsp. milk
- Powdered sugar
- 1 tsp. vanilla
- Nuts

Directions:

1. Combine sugar and flour in a large bowl. Using a heavy saucepan, combine shortening, butter, coffee (or water) and cocoa. Bring to boil and stir well. Pour the boiling mixture over sugar and flour mixture
2. Add buttermilk, baking soda, eggs and vanilla. Mix with an electric mixer on high speed. Pour into a buttered jelly roll pan and bake at 400 degrees F for 20 minutes. Prepare frosting whilst baking.
3. For frosting, boil milk, butter and cocoa in a pan. Add powdered sugar, nuts and vanilla. Apply frosting once brownies are removed from oven.

Apple Cake with Cream Cheese

(ready in about 1 hour 15 minutes | Serving 8)

Ingredients:

- 2 large eggs
- 2 cups of sugar
- 1 cup salad oil
- 1 tsp. vanilla
- 2 cups flour, sifted
- 1 tsp. baking soda
- 1 tsp. cinnamon
- ½ tsp. salt
- 1 cup pecans, chopped
- 4 cups apples, sliced thinly
- **Cream Cheese Icing**
- 2 (3oz) package of cream cheese, softened
- 3 tbsp. melted sweet cream butter

- 2 cups confectionary sugar
- 1 tsp. vanilla

Directions:

1. Beat eggs until foamy. Add oil and sugar, beat for 5 minutes. Combine vanilla, flour, baking soda, salt and cinnamon.
2. Add the apples and nuts, pour batter into a 13x9 inch baking dish, well-greased Bake at 350 degrees F for 50-60 minutes.
3. While baking, mix cream cheese icing ingredients together in a bowl. Allow to cool prior to frosting onto cake.
4. Remove from oven and allow to sit for 10 minutes. Remove from pan and frost with cream cheese icing.

Old Fashion Texas Cherry Dumplings
(ready in about 30 minutes | Serving 6)

Ingredients:

- 1 (16oz) can of sour cherries
- ¾ cup of sugar
- Dumpling batter
- **For Dumpling Batter**
- 1 cup cake flour, sifted
- 1 tsp. baking powder
- ¼ tsp. salt
- ¼ cup of sugar
- Rind of 1 orange, grated
- ½ whole milk
- 2tsp. melted sweet cream butter

Directions:

1. Place undrained cherries and sugar in a wide pan with lid, cover and bring to boil.
2. Combine all dumpling ingredients together and blend well. Drop 1 tbsp. of batter into boiling fruit, one at a time, should make 6 dumplings overall. Cover and cook for 20 minutes
3. Serve with ice cream and enjoy

Tasty Fruit Cobbler
(ready in about 45 minutes | Serving 4-6)

Ingredients:

- ¼ lb. butter
- ½ tsp. salt
- 1 cup flour
- ½ cup milk
- ½ cup sugar
- 1 tsp. baking powder
- Approx.1 ½ cups fruit (vary according to preference)

Directions:

1. Preheat oven to 400 degrees F. Using oven, melt butter into a 10x13" baking dish. Combine flour, sugar, baking powder and salt. Add in milk and mix well. Once butter has melted and spread across

bottom of pan, weave batter in the pan, leave space for where the butter shows. Fill spaces with fruit, piled with sugar and syrup. Place cobbler into oven and bake until browned on edges and sugar starts to caramelize, approx. 35 minutes. Add ice cream and serve.

County Line Bourbon Sauce

(ready in about 35 min | Servings 20)

Ingredients:

- 2 lbs butter
- 2 lbs brown sugar
- 2 cups heavy whipping cream
- 1/3 cup jack daniels bourbon

Directions:

1. Over medium heat, place heavy pan on stove. Melt butter.
2. Break up pieces of brown sugar, add slowly to melted butter. Whisk until sugar is dissolved and mixture is

smooth, just before point of simmering. Reduce or remove from heat if simmering starts to occur.
3. Add heavy whipping cream and stir continuously. Blend well and remove from heat. Add the jack daniels bourbon
4. Whip and mix well before serving.

Texas Chainsaw Barbecue Sauce

(ready in about 1 hour | Servings 8)

Ingredients:

- 2 tbsp. butter
- 1 medium onion, chopped finely
- 2 garlic, minced
- ½ cup orange juice
- 1 cup cider vinegar
- 2 tbsp. fresh lemon juice
- 2 slices lemon
- 1 cup maple syrup
- ¼ cup Worcestershire sauce
- 2 cups ketchup
- ¼ cup molasses
- ¼ cup brown sugar
- 2 tbsp. dry mustard

- 1 tsp. salt
- ½ tsp. red pepper flakes
- ½ tsp. ground cumin
- ½ tsp. paprika

Directions:

1. Using a large saucepan, melt butter over medium heat. Add garlic and onion; cook for 5 minutes, until tender. Stir in cider vinegar, orange juice, lemon juice, lemon slices, Worcestershire sauce, maple syrup, molasses and brown sugar. Season with salt, dry mustard, red pepper flakes, paprika and cumin. Simmer for between 45-60 minutes. Remove lemon slices prior to serving.

Conclusion

Texas has a cooking style all to itself. The main focus of summer foods revolves around barbecuing and smoking foods. Spring, summer and fall are times that you should spend with your family and friends outdoors, enjoying home cooked foods that were slow cooked and delicious.

Purchasing a smoker can be confusing, especially if this is not the type of background that you grew up in. However, we have taken the time to break down the smoker that provides the best quality food and flavor to give you that true Texas flavor that you are looking for. We have also included three amazing sauces that are specially linked to Texas and cannot be found elsewhere.

We truly hope you enjoy the 27 recipes that are included in this book, including the secret Texas sauces that are so delicious they will win your heart and the hearts of your guests.

Copyright: Published in the United States by Daniel K. Hinkle /
© Daniel K. Hinkle

All rights Reserved. No part of this publication or the information in it may be quoted from or reproduced in any form by means such as printing, scanning, photocopying or otherwise without prior written permission of the copyright holder.

Disclaimer and Terms of Use: Effort has been made to ensure that the information in this book is accurate and complete, however, the author and the publisher do not warrant the accuracy of the information, text and graphics contained within the book due to the rapidly changing nature of science, research, known and unknown facts and internet. The Author and the publisher do not hold any responsibility for errors, omissions or contrary interpretation of the subject matter herein. This book is presented solely for motivational and informational purposes only